Copywriting For Beginners:

How To Write, Persuade & Sell Anything To Anyone Like A Pro With Copy!

Table of Contents

Copyright

contained within is the solitary and utter responsibility of the recipient reader. Under no circumstances will any legal responsibility or blame be held against the publisher for any reparation, damages, or monetary loss due to the information herein, either directly or indirectly. Respective authors own all copyrights not held by the publisher.

The information herein is offered for informational purposes solely, and is universal as so. The presentation of the information is without contract or any type of guarantee assurance.

The trademarks that are used are without any consent, and the publication of the trademark is without permission or backing by the trademark owner. All trademarks and brands within this book are for clarifying purposes only and are the owned by the owners themselves, not affiliated with this document.

Introduction

I want to thank you and congratulate you for purchasing this book, *"Copywriting For Beginners: How To Write, Persuade & Sell Anything To Anyone Like A Pro With Copy!"*

This book contains tips to help you start out on a career in copywriting.

You might be wondering if you have what it takes to become a copywriter.

If you are reading this book, you already have one of the most important qualities needed to become a copywriter – curiosity!

Keep on reading and you will find out whether you are more suited to be a technical, content, or creative copywriter; if your strength lies in creating blog posts, press releases, or eBooks; if your skills allow you to have a better shot at providing all kinds of copywriting projects; or if you might be better off specializing on one or two writing jobs.

You will get first-hand information on common mistakes that copywriters are guilty of. Moreover, you will be given tips on how to avoid them. But most importantly, you will have the chance to learn the secrets to becoming a successful copywriter!

Chapter 1: What it takes to be a Copywriter?

At the heart of copywriting is advertising. But far from the blatant hard sell you might encounter from an aggressive salesperson, a copywriter presents all the important details in an informative and an enjoyable format – this is what encourages readers to become potential customers.

You have what it takes to be a copywriter if the following qualities describe you:

1. Passionately Curious. A copywriter has an innate need to always know why. This characteristic is what allows him to enlighten himself on many different subjects. It gives him a chance to educate others as well.

This goes hand in hand with having the passion to write about everything under the sun. Passion is what makes a copywriter believe that every little thing is an interesting subject waiting to be written about.

2. Practices Self-motivation. Given that a copywriter has to work on many different tasks at the same time, he should have the drive to work as efficiently as possible. This is easy to accomplish if he is able to motivate himself. He knows that he cannot expect his clients or employers to inspire him to write.

3. Shows Flexibility. Working as a copywriter requires the ability to easily handle multiple assignments that may or may not belong to the same category. Accomplishing them lets a copywriter's writing skills shine and gives him an opportunity to hone them as well.

4. Master of Conciseness. It takes knowing how to use plain English words to be a good copywriter. He doesn't have to resort to using highfalutin words – a great copywriter does not want to sound pompous and turn off his readers.

It also helps when a copywriter has mastered the art of keeping things as short as possible. A great copywriter is able to inform and entertain his readers even when he goes straight to the point.

5. Great Storyteller. A copywriter may write to sell things, but this does not mean that he will produce an article that has "commercial" stamped all over it. He always strives to put an enjoyable narrative spin on his works.

6. Writer at Heart. A copywriter truly loves what he does for a living and does not mind putting in extra hours, if that is what it takes for him to deliver a well-written article. He also knows that his efforts are not wasted on projects that might have been rejected. Instead, he treats them as opportunities to improve on his writing skills.

7. Focused in Multitasking. Copywriters do not have the luxury of time and this is why it would help them to stay in the moment and set their minds on the writing projects at hand. This is especially important in a job where multitasking is a necessity.

A copywriter who is just starting out cannot avoid multitasking. He can't afford to turn down writing jobs outright, even if it means having to do several projects simultaneously. A great copywriter sees multitasking as a chance to showcase his writing abilities to his employer.

8. Open to Criticisms. On one hand, a great copywriter is confident enough to justify his work if he feels that he is not getting the right feedback for it. On the other hand, he also understands that his job involves having his share of criticisms from clients and editors.

A good copywriter knows it is to his advantage when clients and editors call his attention to mistakes, more so if they give him pointers on how to correct them. This means they want to continue working with him, which is why they are giving him the chance to redeem himself.

9. Enthusiastic Reader. A great copywriter reads as much as he can, knowing that reading is his tool for sharpening his writing skills. He understands that he should not limit himself to topics of interest alone. But then the mere fact that a copywriter enjoys reading in itself allows him to become an expert in writing on a wide range of subjects.

10. Grammar Savvy. A copywriter learns that having the passion to write will not be enough to sustain him in his job. He understands that constantly working to improve his grammar skills is a key to his success in copywriting.
Still, the grammar savvy copywriter knows that perfection is impossible. He will readily acknowledge having committed some grammar lapses from time to time.

Moreover, he knows that it does not pay to be complacent about his job. Honing his grammar skills will give him an edge over other copywriters!

Chapter 2: Types of Copywriter

A lot of different types of products and services are being launched in the market everyday. This is the primary reason why copywriters are in great demand. There are various specializations of copywriters as well. Take a look at the following and see which type you are best suited for:

Technical Copywriter

User manuals and FAQs are the works of art of the technical writer.

Good Grasp
A technical copywriter has a thorough knowledge on a particular field of expertise. It would be difficult for other types of writers, or copywriters for that matter, to write an article on genetic engineering without studying the subject thoroughly. A technical copywriter, on the other hand, can do the job effortlessly.

Piece of Cake
This is the reason why a lot of technical writers do not count as professional writers. Instead, they are professionals in their own fields. A chemist would be able to write an article about The Importance of Chemistry without much difficulty. In the same vein, an engineer would have no qualms about composing an essay on The Best

Architectural Designs within minutes.

A Shot at Creativity
Don't worry – this does not mean you don't stand a chance of becoming a technical copywriter based on your lack of professional training in these fields. You actually have an edge over these experts when your mind is not saturated with technicalities that can hamper creativity in writing.

For example, you could write about Why Chemistry Rocks or Home Designs to Blow Your Mind, which sound much better than the chemist's and the engineer's articles.

A Chance at Rubbing Elbows
On that note, becoming a technical copywriter means you get to work with the technical professionals themselves. You'll find yourself gathering ideas from lawyers, engineers, and computer programmers to use in creating useful articles that will attract your target audience.

You also have the advantage of charging a higher amount for your articles due to the amount of research and concerted effort poured into it.

Content Copywriter

Product scripts are the specialties of the content copywriter.

Good Command
A content copywriter knows how to maneuver his way around words to make his how-to articles sound serious and engaging at the same time. This is an important skill to have if you desire to go into copywriting that involves the presentation of facts about a product in a logical manner. The copy, nonetheless, should be easy and interesting to read.

Target Sighted
A content copywriter strives to write on a single topic and turn out articles with different angles. The articles he produces will then be used in different websites that are targeted toward different types of customers.

Lure Them In

Content copywriting aims to update a particular website on a regular basis by providing the information that answers the concerns of a visitor of that website. But, the job of the copywriter does not end there. He has to make the viewer interested enough to keep reading until he soon becomes a potential customer of the product or service endorsed by that site.

Step By Step

How to use a certain product is the main thrust of content copywriting. The steps are provided in a manner that is easy to understand and that can be followed by the customers without much effort. This is why it is important to engage the reader so that he does not lose interest and move on to other websites instead.

Get Inside Their Heads

The importance of providing useful information in content copywriting cannot be stressed enough. You have to know who will read your articles, how they might react to your content, and why they respond in a certain manner to the ideas you have given to them.

SEO Copywriter

Blog posts and articles are what make up an SEO copywriter's arsenal.

High Visibility
The SEO copywriter is a master in the art of turning out blog posts that are tailored to rank high in internet searches.

Whether the purpose of these articles is to inform or to make an endorsement, the important thing is to write them in a surefire way that lands them a top spot in any search engine result's first page. This ensures that a website will get the exposure it needs to promote its products and services.

Wide Reach
Your value as an SEO copywriter also lies in your ability to draw in a huge number of potential customers to a website. Your articles enable a particular product to get noticed by people from all walks of life and on a global scale.

Highly Reputed
Being an SEO copywriter means you provide your client a great way to advertise its product without having to invest a huge capital. You are giving your client an opportunity to build a great reputation around the internet without spending that much because of your high ranking articles.

Exclusive Service

Undeniably, your greatest contribution as an SEO copywriter is giving your client a means of having an advertising venue that works for him every minute of the day. Your articles give him a big advantage in enticing potential customers to buy his products and services.

Chapter 3: Which Type of Copywriter Are You?

In the previous chapter, you learned about the necessary skills involved in technical, content, and SEO copywriting.

This chapter will show you why creative writing and sales copywriting may be the two most interesting jobs you can aspire to have!

Creative Copywriter

Press releases are the creative copywriter's forte!

Short and Sweet

A creative copywriter possesses a great talent in grabbing a reader's attention with his use of snappy titles and memorable headlines. The ease with which the creative copywriter is able to capture the readers' imagination and drum up their interest in wanting to learn about a new product are what makes him an important asset in any company.

Power of Persuasion

Your ability to weave wonderful words and unify them in a persuasive article is what makes you stand out among other copywriters.

You are able to conceptualize great ideas that give readers a sense of urgency and a need to buy a certain product.   This allows your client to rest assured that they will gain a high number of potential customers.

Marketing Skills

You may have an experience in marketing and this is what helps you deliver well-thought-out articles that are meant to entice readers. Or you may just possess a natural talent in marketing.

What is important is that it is hardly an effort for you to make any type of product or service sound more interesting and marketable.

Heart of the Matter

It cannot be denied that your good command of words which drives readers to become potential customers is an indispensable tool in any business.

However, you should not forget to make sure that your articles are relevant to a customer's needs and are able to deliver accurate details of a product.

Sales Copywriter

eBooks are the sales copywriter's masterpieces!

Multiple Personalities

Sales copywriting has to be the most interesting form of copywriting in the land of advertising. It gives you a chance to play different roles – writer, salesperson, and even psychologist.

Fear of Missing Out

You have a rare talent of making your readers feel that if they don't finish reading your article, then they are missing out on something important to them. Moreover, you have the uncanny ability to leave them wanting to know more about a certain product, and then make them desperate enough to buy it.

Drive into Action

Creative copywriting allows you to provide articles that are able to sell products and services in a persuasive manner – without sounding pushy. Readers hate it when they start reading an article in the hopes that they become informed or entertained, only to find out down the middle that a blatant commercial is waiting to be thrust into their faces. A good sales copywriter does not write anything that makes his readers feel cheated.

The Best of Many Worlds

Creative copywriting is a great avenue for you to produce articles that are able to impress your reader with the unique way you have with words (although this should not be your primary purpose). It also gives you a chance to tug at their emotions and to allow themselves to be persuaded that they absolutely need to have the service or product you just happened to mention in your writing.

Chapter 4: Key Elements of Copywriting?

Because a copywriter often has to play multiple roles at once – technical writer, content provider, SEO ranking generator, creative author, and sales specialist – it's easy to lose sight of the basic rules in effective copywriting.

Here are the things you can't afford to forget:

Adaptability

It goes without saying that a copywriter basically knows all there is to learn about rules on vocabulary, punctuation, and grammar. However, this is not a guarantee that he is an effective one. The English language is written differently in every country.

For example, US writes "color," while UK spells it "colour." Both US and UK also differ in the way they write titles, date, time, and quotations.

Problem Solving

Clients have problems that need solutions – solutions that they are willing to pay for to have someone else get it for them.

They may need someone to create and maintain their blog sites, update their social media accounts, or make sure that their website ranks high in the internet search engines. One of your tasks as a copywriter is to present yourself as the solution that a client should not miss out on.

Meanwhile, readers have needs as well that are waiting to be fulfilled. Some examples of these are learning how to keep their homes clutter-free or knowing how to keep the romance in their marriage alive. You have the power to provide the solutions to their problems. Your self-help eBooks (such as this one) and list articles in blog posts help you have a huge following of readers.

Focus

To say that a copywriter has many ideas is an understatement. You may find yourself having too many ideas in your head that you just have to unload them by writing them down.

However, this tendency of having too many thoughts makes it hard for you to focus on one topic alone. The result is that you might add in ideas onto a certain topic to make it more interesting. In the end you might end up producing an article that sounds senseless because of its lack of a clear line of thought.

Your best bet is to have a focal point in all of your writing projects to ensure that the reader gets what he wants out them.

Perfection (Almost)

This is where having other pairs of eyes to review your finished work comes in handy. You'll benefit from their ability to look at your article with fresh eyes and to easily spot your mistakes. Furthermore, readers are more likely to think that a writer is not serious about what he writes in general if they find even just one article of his that has too many errors in it.

Credibility

Your English instructor was right: research – lots of it – is the key to writing a decent article that will not only add to the wow factor for your readers' benefit but will also satisfy your client's wishes on how the article should turn out. Just remember to reference everything to protect yourself from possible legal issues.

Respect for Your Client

You might be tempted to impress your client with the article you agreed to deliver to him by adding in some interesting facts (which may be unrelated, but are awesome.) that are not specified in the project details.

Wrong move: Clients would much rather you followed their instructions to the letter than have you tampering with their wishes.

Purpose

Jumping from one topic to the next within an article makes it sound as though you have too many great ideas to be able to stick to just one. The truth is, you might just be deluding yourself – your readers might have a different perception. What your readers are more likely to believe is that you are a writer who lacks organization and who has not prepared an outline.

You should write your articles in a manner that leaves your readers interested and makes them impatient to know what is about to follow. The last thing you want is to have your readers finally understand what you're driving at only by the time they reach the end of your article.

Inspiration

You know you've done a great job in copywriting when you are able to inspire your readers to feel a host of emotions, the most important of which is fear.

Readers are more likely to buy the product or service you are selling in your article if they feel afraid of losing something. For example, your topic might be about hair loss, and because you were successful in inspiring the sense of fear in your readers, they will end up buying the hair loss solution you have written about.

Simplicity

When copywriting, it helps to always keep things simple. An article that is simply written allows your readers to understand your messages in one go. For instance, since time is such a rare luxury nowadays, eBooks were created to make the act of reading more convenient.

Respect for Your Readers

You show respect to your readers when you spare them from reading highly technical words that give them eyestrain while reading your content. You also show your readers that you care about them by stating your message in your article immediately and giving them a chance to avoid being bored while reading.

Chapter 5: Mistakes to Avoid in Copywriting?

Revisions and rejections are all part of a copywriter's job. After all, it is impossible to deliver the perfect article all the time, if at all. Nobody wants to have their efforts in writing go to waste. This is why it is important to always go back to the basics.

It's Too Complicated

Whether you are working freelance or as a permanent hire, copywriting is still a job that requires professionalism. To be a professional writer means to stop yourself from showing off your excellent grammar and spelling skills. It's best to keep your language as simple as possible. Your readers will thank you for it by reading your piece up to the end.

Wrong Punctuation

In the hopes of avoiding the risk of sounding long-winded, even great copywriters might commit the use of wrong punctuations. The incorrect placement of the em-dash or a comma within a sentence can create an awkward pause while reading it. Having a punctuation guide on standby would be helpful.

Too Technical

Copywriting strives to reach the highest possible number of potential customers, so any attempt to use highly technical words wouldn't be worth it. You might be surprised to find out that even technical people would find it easier to read an article that is not wallowing in excessive use of jargons.

Wrong Mindset

A copywriter can sometimes lose sight of the fact that the main purpose of his job is to write something that would benefit his readers. One highly possible reason for this lapse is the inclination to write on subjects that interest him to ensure that he delivers a great article every time, even without the benefit of lots of research work.

If these subjects do not offer any value to his readers, all the efforts he poured into writing them would just be a waste of time.

Letting It Go

Forgetting to place a call-to-action feature in your article would render it useless. In fact, failing to include a call to action would have to be the greatest mistake that any copywriter can commit.

Your job as a copywriter does not only involve letting readers know about a particular service or product. You have to do all the necessary steps to make them interested in buying it.

Do your best to create a message that sounds too urgent to be overlooked by your readers. Then make certain that explicit instructions are included in your article as to how they can purchase the product mentioned.

Chapter 6: Keys to Success in Copywriting?

You have determined that you do have what it takes to become a copywriter. You have also identified which type of copywriter you ought to be. Moreover, you have discovered the basics to remember and the mistakes to avoid in copywriting. Now, it is time for you to learn the secrets in becoming successful at it!

Mind the Rules in Writing -Write in the Second Person

Copywriters have to follow specific rules in writing, one of which is writing in the second person. This is a significant shift from what we learned in English class – the standard way of writing is almost always in the third person.

Because copywriting is a form of advertising, you have to assume the role of a salesperson. Writing in the second person lets you accomplish that. Conditioning your mind to always consider the angle of selling to your readers will make it easier for you to do your tasks as a copywriter.

Use the Active Voice

Copywriting is a business that involves selling, so there is no use in being reluctant in your writing style. Subtle suggestions have no place in your articles. You need to get your readers to take action after they read your written work.

For example, you have to write "Read this" on a sales letter, and "Open now" on a direct mail envelope. The words do sound obvious, but that is the whole purpose of placing them there. You have to make sure that the people who will receive it won't have to second-guess anything.

Never Give Up

There are a lot of copywriting opportunities nowadays that it is almost impossible not to come up with a single lead. In fact, you have it easier compared to past generations of copywriters. You literally have the whole world at your fingertips. Applying for jobs online is definitely more convenient than knocking on every office door in town.

You may not immediately find a job once you send your applications online. But it helps to think that it is much better to wait until you land a job where you fit right in with the company culture than to force yourself in a job that may only last for a couple of months because you don't blend in with the agency's work climate.

Be Ready for a Writing Test

Even if you have been writing all your life, preparing for a writing test might still cause you to feel nervous. Don't worry: just keep in mind that a test is given to gauge your writing skills, not to cause you pain. Focus on gaining knowledge before the day of the test.

It will truly help you to read on a lot of reading materials on a certain topic before taking the test. You could be asked to write an article within a two-hour time frame, so practice doing this as often as you can. A great way to practice writing is to find an article online that deals with the test topic and to rewrite the whole thing in your own words. Always remember to avoid plagiarism.

Expect to Start Small

At the start of your career in copywriting, it would be expected that you have to experience a lot of hard work and to receive low pay. The advantage that you have in this setup is the opportunity to gain more writing experience which hones your skills in the process.

Like a great number of copywriters, you have to start at a small rate. After a few months, when you have already experienced writing on different types of articles and have learned tips on improving your skills, you'll find your rates getting higher.

Use Your Passion for Writing

Copywriting involves creating a number of different articles, each of which has specific instructions as to how they should be written – and you have to accomplish them in a short time while keeping in mind that your articles have to meet the standards set by your employer and your clients.

Your job does require you to put in long hours in reading, writing, and proofreading, and you also have to sacrifice some personal needs. But as someone who truly has a passion for writing, all the hard work does not feel like work at all. In fact, you can see yourself doing this job for the rest of your life, if possible.

Happy writing!

Conclusion

Thank you again for purchasing this book!

I hope this book was able to help you reinforce your resolve to become a successful copywriter!

The next step is to keep coming back to the key elements of copywriting, to always remember the mistakes to avoid as a copywriter, and to consistently apply the secrets to achieving success in your chosen career.

Rest assured that you have numerous opportunities at your disposal as a copywriter. Just bear in mind that not all copywriters are the same, so it is important that you make the decision to become a general copywriter or to focus on one specialty.

Thank you and best of success!

Bonus Content

As a token of our appreciation Grand Reveur Publications would like to give you access to our exclusive bonus content (including free eBooks!).

Exclusive pre-release access to our latest eBooks Free Grand Reveur eBooks during promotional periods

A method ANYONE can use to publish their own book and make passive income

To receive this bonus content please visit the following web site:

https://ignorelimits.leadpages.net/grandreveur publications/

As this is a limited time offer it would be a shame to miss out, I recommend grabbing these bonuses before reading on.